Argosy of Sail

Argosy of Sail

A Photographic History
of Sail

CLIFFORD W. HAWKINS

Collins

AUCKLAND   SYDNEY   LONDON

Books by the same author
The Log of the Huia
A Maritime Heritage
(Revised version of *Out of Auckland*)
The Dhow

First published 1980
William Collins Publishers Ltd
Box 1, Auckland

© 1980 Clifford W. Hawkins
ISBN 0 00 216964 9 ✓

Typeset by Jacobson Typesetters, Auckland
Printed in Hong Kong

Contents

Preface

THIS PHOTOGRAPHIC BIOGRAPHY represents over forty-five years spent pursuing sailing ships with a camera. During that time I have studied some of man's earliest water craft and followed their development from log raft through to the latter-day sailing ship. Thus, through the medium of my own photography, I am able to portray some two thousand years of sail. So antiquated are some of the vessels I have studied that at times I have felt as if I were taking part in the sea-life of centuries long past.

There are few posed photographs in these pages and any attempt at composition has usually taken place only at the darkroom stage of producing a print — if at all. I see these pictures from an historian's point of view rather than that of an artistic photographer. Yet I may have compromised here and there especially where there is emphasis on the sea or the reflected image rather than on the ship itself. In any case, rarely can one study such things as composition from a moving boat and when the subject is also in motion. Again, the pursuing boat is often a working one with her own specific task to perform, so that the photographer is the last consideration of her master. Much of my photography has been a catch as catch can game of chance which has given me an excellent excuse for not conforming with other people's ideas of what makes a picture. My purpose in carrying a camera has been primarily to make a pictorial record of ships and shipping, although I have never ignored an opportunity to produce a seascape.

I have taken hundreds of photographs of powered vessels but none appear here apart from those of auxiliary sailing ships and the occasional interloper in the background that could not be avoided. It was impossible to eliminate the *Naess Venturer* for instance, or the intrusion of *Prinsesse Margrethe*. The presence of these vessels, however, does serve to emphasise the evolution in sea transport that caused the demise of sail. But, who knows, the day may well dawn when sail is once more in the ascendancy and even now I would not be at all surprised if those Levant schooners have outlasted the *Naess Venturer*, and with the continued love and care bestowed upon the *Isefjord* that vessel too may well be sailing out of Copenhagen long after *Prinsesse Margrethe* has gone into retirement.

I hope that in future years this personal record of the world's sailing craft will be treasured as much for the medium in which it has been printed as for the subject it portrays.

Cliff Hawkins

From the Beginning

Ranking with the coracle as one of the oldest forms of water transport still in use is the catamaran — the 'tied logs' of Sri Lanka. This crude fishing craft can be seen at Negombo, a short distance north of Colombo. It consists merely of several shaped logs, usually four, bound together with lashings made from coconut fibre.

On such a raft a lone fisherman has just enough space to stow his net and any fish he may catch. Larger craft are sometimes put together by using a greater number of logs. A single spritsail is set from two bamboo spars stepped in V formation. When sailing on the wind the tack of this sail is taken forward and the clew to a position aft. The only standing rigging consists of backstays, one from the head of each spar. A sweep is employed for steering but in the photograph taken in 1959 the fisherman improvises with a length of bamboo. When a catamaran becomes waterlogged the components are simply taken apart and dried out in the sun.

At Negombo I was to witness yet another phase in man's progress towards actual boatbuilding: the dugout canoe having strakes fastened to it with coconut-fibre stitching. Fitted with an outrigger for stability this produces what is known as the oru. This craft also brings into use the leeboard to counter drift when under sail. These are visible in the photograph of the canoes drawn up on the ocean beach at Negombo, but what has yet to come into use is a method of changing course by tacking. The oru does not go about. In changing from one board to the other the V mast assembly is twisted round and the backstays shifted to the other end of the hull. The bow is now the stern, and without any further ado the

canoe begins to gather way on its new board or course.

Still at Negombo, there is to be seen another type of fishing craft, the pedar or peter boat built with thin planking above a base of shaped logs. Such a manner of construction persists not only in Sri Lanka but across the Gulf of Mannar and far along the Malabar Coast of India. That which I came across at Dona Paula Bay in Goa provides a fine example of 'sewn' planking built up from a dugout log base. Little did I then know that on this coast trading vessels built entirely of planks sewn together with coconut fibre were, in this day and age, still in commission.

At Negombo the way of life is just as it must have been many centuries ago, with the fisherfolk gaining their livelihood from the sea in their primitive craft while the peasant farmers ashore tilled the land with implements of a remote age. These people are extremely poor, especially when compared with many of their compatriots in industry. Yet maybe in their meagre existence they probably find greater contentment. Out on the ocean's wide expanse, far from the daily social strife, there is a real tranquillity.

In this part of the world Nature can still provide all that a fisherman needs. The use of a length of bamboo for a steering oar is not an improvisation. An oru hull is shaped from logs, bamboos form the spars, coconut fibre is made up into the lashings, and rigging and sails are cut from locally-made materials. When the south-west monsoon arrives the Sri Lankan needs no umbrella: he simply cuts a banana leaf and places it over his head so that the rainwater drains away behind him as if from a gutter. This is the world to which the catamaran and oru belong.

A lone fisherman of Sri Lanka. His catamaran is one of man's most primitive forms of watercraft still in use (Negombo 1959)

The logs of the catamaran are taken apart for drying out. An outrigger canoe plys as a ferry on the lagoon. *Below*, the oru represents one of the earliest examples of boatbuilding with strakes stitched to a base log and an outrigger for stability (Negombo 1959)

The pedar fishing boat of Sri Lanka is built up from a number of base logs and so has a greater beam than the oru. There is no outrigger (Negombo 1959). *Below*, a stitched craft built up from a dugout base log (Dona Paula near Panaji, Goa 1972)

The Nile Felucca

WITH THE SECOND NEW ZEALAND EXPEDITIONARY FORCE in 1940 I was based in Egypt, first at Maadi and then at Helwan. Here was an excellent opportunity to study the feluccas on the Nile whenever leave permitted it. No one appeared to be concerned whether photography on the river contravened wartime regulations or not but, knowing that the Cairo bridges were a sensitive area, I kept away from them. South of the metropolis all was peaceful, and I could chase feluccas to my heart's content. On the banks of the Nile one was completely free from the tension of war.

The felucca is the traditional craft of the Nile basin and is one of the few vessels that carries the true three-cornered lateen sail. Its tall tapering yard remains in the hoisted position, and to set sail an agile youngster must be sent scampering aloft to loosen the robands and again to put the sail into stops at journey's end. One day, while crossing the river by felucca to Saqqara, our course converged with that of a southbound lateener. Also under sail, we were able to cut under its bows and so secure the beautiful photograph of 2357.

The lateen sail as seen in the felucca was common right through the Mediterranean from Spain to the Levant. As late as the nineteenth century Spanish pinks and xebecs set lateen sails on as many as three masts.

But it is not definitely known where the rig originated. There is a theory that it was introduced to the Mediterranean and European seafarers by the Arabs, possibly before the eighth century. The lateen, including the Arabian settee with its short fore-edge or luff, is the ideal sail in areas where a reliable steady wind is a certainty; but where storms and squalls persist it can be an awkward and indeed a dangerous one to handle. It is a wonder that such a sail was in use for so long in the. Mediterranean, where sudden squalls of extreme violence are commonplace at certain times of the year. Eventually the sail was com-

In the land of the Pharoahs the felucca, with its Mediterranean lateen sail, adds beauty to the Nile scene
(Helwan 1941)

12

bined with square rig and it was taken back to Arabian waters by the Portuguese when they established trade with the Indies.

The beauty of the felucca is almost entirely dependent upon its lofty lateen sails. The hull is little more than a flat-bottomed barge, but to compensate for lack of sheer the planking comes up to a spectacular high apex in the bows so that, after all, this hardworking craft does possess an individual characteristic not altogether displeasing to the eye.

At Cairo's Old Port feluccas by the score nudged into the riverbank. Such a scene might well be imagined as set in another age but, despite the mechanisation of the major part of Egypt's transport system, these ancient craft, unfettered by any modern laboursaving devices, disgorged produce on the lowered backs of the stevedores.

It is a strange fact of life that the sailing ship, recognised as one of the most beautiful of man's technical achievements, has survived only where sweated labour exists. Yet the crews of these vessels and, as I was to see later, those of the Arabian and Indian dhows, live under far better conditions than many of the countless poor who dwell ashore with or without employment. Certainly it is no light task stemming the river's flow with nothing more than a weighty sweep. But there are moments of rest, perhaps in the shade of a scented mimosa tree, while a felucca drifts by in reflections of the moment.

Aboard a Nile ferry it would not be unusual for a passenger to compete with a donkey for deck space. Here time rather than a timetable contributes to an efficient service unhindered by the complications of a more sophisticated society.

Manpower helps in the absence of a breeze (Cairo 1942). *Right*, making for Cairo (Helwan 1941) and *below right*, solace in the shade of a mimosa (Maadi 1941)

Reaching for the sky the sail of this felucca is able to catch a little more of the gentle zephyr coming off the hot sand (Nile 1941) and *below*, reflections in the Nile (Helwan 1941). *Right*, off Memphis the feluccas are close to an area of great archaeological significance (Nile 1941)

Onion crop discharging from feluccas and *below*, the crowded port of Old Cairo. *Right*, fodder comes ashore on the backs of stevedores (Cairo 1941)

Feluccas under construction (Cairo 1941)

20

The Nile ferry (Helwan 1941)

East of Suez

It WAS AT ADEN in 1939 that I first caught sight of Arab dhows. Lying off Ma'alla was a fleet of two-masted baghlas, booms and sambuks, while inshore many smaller sambuks and zarooks canted over on their bilges.

Few vessels have such a lineage as the dhow. They are the descendants of craft that traded in the Arabian Sea long before European intrusion, and whose timbers were fastened together with dowels and coir. The double-ended booms and zarooks were representatives of the older form of hull construction. The transom stern as seen in the baghla and sambuk did not come into vogue until the square-sterned European vessels appeared in the Arabian Sea.

Aden's Ma'alla shipyard was reputed to be the oldest in the world still in use, but since my first photographs of dhows were taken there in 1939 the construction of a motorway has caused the yard to be shifted to another site close to the Slave Island causeway. The historic connection no longer exists. The dhows coming to Ma'alla have also become fewer in recent years. The baghlas and certain other types of dhow have become extinct, and since most of those that survive are now engined they step but a single mast carrying a small sail of questionable value. I consider myself fortunate in having seen the older type of sambuk not only under construction in the Ma'alla yard but also under sail, now a rare sight in Arabian waters.

Zarooks as well as sambuks regularly call at Aden and even though they too are motorised their hull form remains much the same as when they voyaged under sail alone. The zarook is a double-ended craft with its raking stem and the sternpost both terminating abruptly externally about halfway up from the waterline. This peculiarity of construction has always been associated with the zarook, right from the time when Europeans first set eyes on these strange craft. What has disappeared though is the old method of steering with ropes attached to a yoke and toggles. This can now be seen only in the few remaining bedans from east of the Hadhramaut.

The sambuk is distinguished from other dhows by its curved stem terminating in a deep plank with a concave inboard end. The transom stern is less ornately carved these days, as are the quarter strakes with their runs of 'rope twist' moulding, reflecting what must be the effects of present-day economies. Unlike the zarook, which is freely decorated with colourful geometric arabesques and strakes painted from stem to stern, the sambuk is almost devoid of paintwork. In many such dhows a lone star and a crescent, or a scimitar painted at the stemhead, suffice in the way of colourwork. The hull is periodically smeared in shark oil, and no vessel but a dhow built of teak could look any smarter after receiving such a treatment.

Dhows at Aden (1939) and *right*, a sambuk from Somalia (off Aden 1959)

Ma'alla; shipwright and *below*, caulking (Aden 1972). *Right*, a sambuk nears completion and *below right*, a new machuwa, (1972)

South to Zanzibar

ALTHOUGH TIMES HAVE CHANGED since Vasco da Gama engaged Ahmad ibn Majid to accompany him to India, it is not difficult to imagine what the coast of East Africa was like when little else but dhows entered Lamu, Malindi, Mombasa, and Zanzibar further to the south. Today on the muddy foreshores of these harbours one is still more or less isolated from developments not in keeping with the old dhow trade. At Pwakuu in Mombasa's Old Port the near-ancient craft may still be seen and heard as they are hauled up on the hard to lusty chanting. Here the hulls are cleaned of their growth of green weed and barnacles accumulated during the voyage just ended and given a fresh application of shahamu. This is a mixture of fat and lime boiled together in a big iron pot of the kind that one imagines was used for cannibalistic purposes in 'darkest' Africa. The mixture, smeared over the underwater part of the hull, dries out as a hard encrustment impervious to attack from the teredo.

In Mombasa and Zanzibar visitors are shown relics and sites associated with the slave traffic and it is not difficult to envisage the conditions that prevailed ashore and in the dhows that carried the human freight off to Arab lands.

One of the traditional dhow trading routes was between Arabian ports and East Africa. Each year several hundred sail drifted with the north-east monsoonal wind and a favourable ocean current, following the coast of Africa until they reached distant Mombasa, Zanzibar and the Rufiji. Trading at way ports, picking up and dropping off passengers, it was a leisurely cruise with no necessity to crack on any pace. The return voyage could take place only with the change of the monsoon. Few dhows now take part in this seasonal trek. Racial strife in East Africa and the imposition of trade restrictions have made it uneconomic and even impossible for dhow owners to operate in the traditional manner, and the trade is now all but dead.

At Mombasa in 1972 I was privileged to see two of the last surviving Suri ganjas. This type of South Arabian dhow is the poor relation of the old baghla but carries much less ornamentation on its transom; it makes up for that deficiency with bright arabesque paintwork on the hull about the high poop. Unfortunately these dhows, like so many others, are now motorised and carry very little sail.

The Suri ganja *Jadakarim* at Pwakuu (Mombasa 1972)

Boat crew for the dhows and
below, 'steady as she goes'
(Mombasa 1972). *Right*, fishing
dhows off Zanzibar (1972)

Oman and the Gulf

It is the same story throughout the Arab world: the diesel engine has annihilated sail. Yet here and there one may witness a scene commonly enacted before oil became so all-important in the Middle East. Dhowmen mingling with smugglers; a turbaned Baluchi merchant, a Negro nakhoda; the crowded suq. Such photographic opportunities still go begging. At Matrah, as I was bargaining for a silver filigree jambiya brooch, an Omani band paraded through the narrow byways in celebration of a young couple's marriage.

Muscat and Matrah are exciting places, but changes are taking place even there, and all too soon the most photogenic subjects, including the dhows, will have disappeared. But likely to endure many more years of the torturing Omani climate are the forts built by the Portuguese in the sixteenth century.

Photographing dhows from a canoe off Matrah early one morning I was captivated by the rugged beauty that confronted me. Mountains and fort cast murky shadows in the bay, providing a rare opportunity to photograph some dhows in a setting more typical of the times in which once they traded. After drifting for a while among the dhows everything fell into place. I shot in colour and black-and-white and was well satisfied with the morning's excursion, taking further photographs of the dhows as I headed for the shore.

Matrah comes to life early in the day. As the sun endeavours to penetrate the moisture-laden atmosphere the Omani fishermen come in from the sea to auction their catch on the muddy shore — a filthy place with the nauseating smells of decaying rubbish and human filth rising in a dank vapour. Not only was this the fish market but a public toilet as well. Rarely does a photograph convey any idea of the conditions under which it was taken. The Arabian Nights scene of Dubai certainly looks romantic and so in fact it was; but during the daylight hours on this Trucial Coast the sizzling heat, even in the shade of a date palm, can cause considerable distress — as at Abu Dhabi, when perspiration dripped into my camera and my glasses became hopelessly fogged up while I changed a film. But despite the discomfort of high humidity, the gulf can be most exhilarating with all its photographic possibilities.

I shall always remember one remarkable scene in Kuwait for the photograph it produced. I was walking along the Sief taking note of the dhows drawn up for repair when quite unexpectedly I was confronted by a group of Kuwaitis, all in their traditional white dishdashas, partaking of morning coffee. It was a perfect setting, under an awning, with a dhow very conveniently positioned as a backdrop. But what to do without offending or disturbing such a gathering can pose a problem. Perhaps a chance has to be taken and apologies made later — or should permission to photograph be sought first of all? Then there is the risk that the group might become more posed and unnatural, or the party could break up prematurely to avoid being photographed. Here one must endeavour to observe certain courtesies and not be unnecessarily obtrusive. In taking this photograph I was fortunate in receiving the full cooperation of all those concerned. There was a sense of fellowship between the photographer and those being photographed.

It was Kuwait that first drew me to the Arabian Gulf because it was there that the great baghlas and booms used to be built. These were the two main types of dhow that undertook the annual voyage from the Shatt al Arab and Gulf ports to East Africa, out on the north-east monsoonal wind and home on the south-west change.

Dhows are still being built in Kuwait and at many other places on the Gulf, but they are mostly small booms, balams, shuais and 'launches' — motorised craft with straight stems and transom sterns. Baghlas with their galleried sterns are a thing of the past, and so is the Arab dhow with a decent-sized sail, since the auxiliary engine has relegated propulsion by wind to a secondary position. Even the older dhows that are still in commission have had their sail area considerably reduced on the installation of an engine.

In the dhow harbours of Arabia I was delighted to observe dates arriving from Basrah in the traditional packages made from palm leaves. A dhow's size was always calculated by the number of these packages of dates it could stow.

Auctioning fish on Matrah Beach
(Oman 1972)

Dubai across the Khor from Deira (United Arab Emirates 1967)

Arabian Gulf sunset, Abu Dhabi (1967)

Dhows off Matrah Fort and *below*, an old 'country craft', the
Vanketshwarloo of Bedi at Matrah (Oman 1972)

Dhowman of the Trucial Coast,
Abu Dhabi (United Arab Emirates
1967). *Below*, morning coffee on
the Sief (Kuwait 1972)

India's West Coast

Tᕼɪꜱ ɪꜱ the Malabar Coast, known for its rich trade even before the Chinese sailed their junks to Quilon in the seventh century. By the eighteenth century the Portuguese, Dutch, English, French, Germans, Danes and even Americans were vying with each other for a share of the trade, particularly the purchase of pepper. Cochin, midway between Calicut and Quilon, became the most important centre for the entrepôt trade. Vessels arrived with silk, camphor and porcelain from Macao, cinnamon from Ceylon, copper from Japan, and sugar, cloves and nutmeg from Batavia. These and other commodities from the East enticed merchants from far and wide. There was also a great demand for gunny sacks from Bengal, and each year cotton cloth came in dhows or bombaras from Calicut and the north.

Trade was invariably fraught with considerable danger and anxiety. Monopolies, licences, taxes, subterfuge and intrigue, all had a place in the eternal rivalry between the trading factions, while piratical blockades were a constant source of trouble in the Arabian Sea. The junks from the Far East ceased to trade with Quilon sometime in the sixteenth century, after there had been some friction in Calicut.

The pattern of trade then changed, with Malacca becoming the transhipment port and Malabar dhows carrying the cargoes between the Strait of Malacca and India, although European vessels did carry cargo direct from the Far Eastern ports through to Malabar. Arabian dhows came from distant Mocha and Jeddah in the Red Sea, also from South Arabian ports, from Aden to Muscat. All kinds of dhows, Arab and Indian, carried out the trade in the Arabian Sea area. Bombaras, batels, dinghies and gallevats came from Basrah and the Persian ports as well as from the Sind and Kathiawar. No wonder then that the Malabar Coast is so full of interest.

The West Coast of India is one of the few areas where the sailing ship remains as an indispensable part of the transport system. The trade, however, is seasonal as the whole of the coast is a dangerous lee shore during the south-west monsoon and all but the larger ports are then closed to shipping.

I was in Bombay and Goa in 1972 and decided then that India deserved more of my time, so in the following year I returned. Starting off with a look at the sewn Masula boats at Madras I travelled south to Tuticorin, the home port of the thoni and where that type of dhow continues to be built. From there I went across to Quilon and through the Malabar ports to Bombay.

For me the Malabar Coast was an area of great discovery, especially Beypore with its extensive shipbuilding industry. But most important of all it was there that I came across the completely sewn craft from the Laccadive Islands, the odams of Androth. Boarding one of these dhows was like taking several steps back in maritime history; but later on, at Bombay, I was to encounter another much larger sewn hull in the shape of a pattimar.

This pattimar was all of eighty feet in length and extraordinarily broad of beam, much like a huge misshapen dish, or pear-shaped, according to an early account of these craft. Measurements have shown instances where the breadth was over half the length of the hull between perpendiculars, and such proportions might easily have been the same here.

The hull planking of these big sewn pattimars is also dowelled, nails taking no part in the construction. This oldtimer in Bombay proved that there was nothing fragile about the early Persian craft that were built in a similar manner before the introduction of iron fastenings. She had just arrived in port laden with timber from the Malabar Coast and would make several such voyages during a sailing season.

At Calicut it was my good fortune to sail in a thoni to Beypore; not a very long journey but one of sufficient duration to allow a set of photographs to be obtained in waters of great historic significance. It was off Calicut that Vasco da Gama first sighted India in 1498, and there was I on the very same coast and under sail with a crew who were Roman Catholics. They were Catholics because their forebears had known the Portuguese who brought the faith to India following da Gama's first contact with the subcontinent.

Timber from the Malabar Coast. The pattimar has a stitched hull (Bombay 1973)

Padaos discharging gravel at
Mahim Bay (Bombay 1972). *Below*,
child labour at Panaji (Goa 1972)

Carved transom of the kotia *Al Madina* (Beypore 1973)

Going out to the *Mary Isabel* in
Calicut Roadstead (Calicut 1973)

Manning the capstan aboard the kotia *Salamat* and *below*, kotias from the Maldives moored in Colombo (Colombo 1959)

Thoni and Batel

THE TUTICORIN thoni is a comparatively modern development and must not be confused with the older Jafna thoni from across the Palk Strait. The Indian vessel began its life as a sailing lighter carrying freight between ship and shore because Tuticorin had no berthage for deep-sea vessels. Despite port developments the thoni continues to perform this duty although the older craft, no longer fit for long voyages, are now relegated to the harbour work. New hulls continue to be built at Tuticorin for the West Coast trade.

The thoni from Tuticorin is easily recognised by its double-ended hull, painted black with large white registration numbers at the bows and right aft. There are usually two masts, lateen-rigged on the main and European gaff-rigged on the short mizzen. There are single and three-masters, the latter being lateen-rigged on the fore and main masts. It was aboard one of these, the *Mary Isabel*, that I sailed when on the Malabar Coast during 1973.

Such a great array of sail as set by the Tuticorin thoni is unknown in any other type of dhow and, except for the mizzen gaff-rig, must be the result of Tuticorin inventiveness. The yards, for instance, are not hung in the normal dhow fashion but are mast-headed with tackle and usually kept hoisted when the sails are furled. As the yards cannot be dipped when tacking, one is hung to port and the other to starboard so that one sail pulls clear of its mast while the other is afoul although still performing its task. If there is but a single lateen (settee) sail it is alternately free and foul of the mast. Above the fore (or main) yard an odd-looking topsail is set from a short topmast. In other Indian dhows the tops'l clews are usually taken to the extreme ends of the yard to give the sail a far better spread. Of course in the thoni this would create problems with that extraordinary headsail stretched out with a spar stepped diagonally from the bows: The *Mary Isabel* also set two spritsails from bamboos under the bowsprit, and a watersail under the boom of the mizzen. A great sight this, but commonplace on the west coast of India. Notice too the raffee set above the yard of the *Maria Antoraj*.

Photographing the *Maria Antoraj* as she set out from Bombay for Veraval was made possible by the use of a boat from another thoni and with it a crew of willing and capable youngsters who had instructions to do all that I asked of them. They were prepared to chase anything within sight, and so eager were they to please that when the *Maria Antoraj* came into view they pulled on the oars with all they could give. By the time we reached her the thoni could not have put on another sail. Besides the huge settee she set the raffee above it and a tops'l. Out ahead was the odd-shaped jib and a waters'l from under the sprit, while above the gaff mizzen was a tops'l and below it the waters'l. What a fantastic sight! Everything was right — the lighting, the setting, and the timing. My crew pulled ahead under the bows and then dropped back to windward. This was a run with black-and-white film in the Rolleiflex and colour in the 35mm camera. As we came up on the leeward side again I put colour in the Rollei and we made another circuit.

No sooner was the *Maria Antoraj* finished with than another thoni hove in sight, a three-master inward bound. She had already taken in her tops'l and then in came the monstrous jib. This was a marvellous opportunity to observe the whole operation of one of these vessels shortening sail as she came into port. Up the skying yards scrambled the youngest and more agile members of the crew to put the big settee sails into gaskets as they were brailed in, and when we drew alongside the now almost stationary thoni her name could be made out: *Maria Alexshantha* of Tuticorin. It had been a most satisfying morning and, after photographing a pattimar under sail for good measure, it was all too soon time to return the boat and its crew to the bunder.

Well remembered is the occasion when I chased a batel — on foot. It happened at Panaji in Goa early one morning following a canoe excursion to photograph kotias on the Mandovi River at sunrise. So intensely interested was I in the subject at hand that I had not noticed the sail of a dhow disappearing over the tops of the coconut palms well down the river. I ran through the main street of the town, which for-

The Tuticorin thoni *Maria Antoraj* (Bombay 1973)

tunately had not yet come to life, and along the riverbank until I came within photographic range of my quarry. I was so exhausted after the long run that it was almost impossible to keep my cameras steady for a few pot shots before the batel sailed out of range. I doubt whether I could make such an effort today!

A magnifying glass on the negative reveals the dhow's name as *Safia*, something that I could not discern with the naked eye.

The *Maria Antoraj* from astern (1973)

The thoni *Maria Alexshantha* taking in sail (Bombay 1973). *Below*, the three-masted thoni *Mary Isabel* off Calicut (1973)

45

A batel on the Mandovi River
(Goa 1972). *Left*, the Veraval batel
Ram Prasad (Bombay 1972)

46

A thoni under construction at
Tuticorin, Tamil Nadu (1973).
Below, in a Malabar shipyard
(Beypore 1973)

Hong Kong and Singapore

IN 1976 I passed through Hong Kong and, with the knowledge that few if any of the old junks remained in service, I was quite prepared on arrival at Aberdeen for the disappointment of not finding a single decent Chinese lugsail anywhere in sight. It was raining and an awful stench rose with the foul vapour off the littered shore. But one moment! Let us have a look at the yuloh in action.

The yuloh is the single oar developed by the Chinese as a means of sculling their sampans. At its best it is a finely balanced built-up spar, but it can degenerate to a poor improvisation comprised of a light pole or length of bamboo with a piece of packing-case wood for the blade. What actually makes the yuloh is a line taken from the end of the spar, or the loom, to either a thwart or to the bottom of the sampan so that the spar angles at approximately 45 degrees to the surface of the water.

In the small Hong Kong sampan propulsion is achieved by a sculling motion with both hands on the loom, and even a youngster soon becomes adept at this action. In China the usual method of handling the yuloh is to twist the loom with one hand and simultaneously push and pull the attached taut line with the other.

In foreign waters one cannot fail to notice the varying methods of small boat propulsion. In Malaysia and Singapore, for instance, it is customary to row from a standing position and facing forward so that the sampan, instead of being pulled, is actually pushed. In the photograph it will be noticed that the oars are crossed. The sampan is emerging from under the extended poop of a Singapore trader. Beyond is the bow of a similar vessel with its foremast stepped right in the eyes, so to speak. Besides carrying battened lugsails these craft are equipped with Chinese-type windlasses that have their drums in the horizontal plane.

Singapore became known for its tonkangs. Such vessels were built early in this century for carrying logs from the forests of Malaysia to the mills in Singapore. Not many tonkangs are now in commis-

Sampans at Aberdeen (Hong Kong 1976)

ng with the yuloh (Aberdeen, Hong Kong 1976)

Aberdeen sampans (Hong Kong 1976). *Right*, tonkangs at Kallang, and *below*, under the stern of a Singapore trader (Singapore 1967)

sion for the simple reason that there is little timber-producing forest left across the Johore Strait.

Some years ago a number of tonkangs lay rotting in the shallows near Kallang, but the area is now all reclaimed land. A few tonkangs continue to find employment however and quite recently I saw a Singapore trader with battened lugsails in the Kallang Basin. The tonkang, unlike the 'trader', has a transom stern and that queer latticed bowsprit. The ungainly wall-sided hull is undecked amidships and measures up to ninety feet or more in length with a beam of around thirty feet and a depth of up to fifteen feet making it possible to stow an enormous load of logs. There is the usual long overhanging poop structure, so typical of Malaysian craft, providing accommodation for the crew. It is really little more than a verandah cantilevered out from the hull proper. The rig is that of a pole-masted ketch with standing gaffs. The mainsail is loose-footed but the mizzen clew is secured to the end of a boom. A staysail and two jibs complete the sail plan.

Starved for anything more attractive I was compelled to photograph the tonkangs as they spent their last days rotting in the mud as the home of hordes of cockroaches, which obviously found the odious débris lying about conducive to their style of living.

At one time Singapore was crowded with all manner of sailing craft but, as in Hong Kong, their numbers have dwindled until now there is very little left to attract the photographer unless he is interested in modern shipping. For that both Hong Kong and Singapore are superb.

At Singapore there is a small maritime museum on Sentosa Island, run by the Port of Singapore Authority. It contains a number of small Malaysian boats as well as a display of models of local craft. The museum is pleasantly sited in a maritime park reached either by a soaring aerial cablecar or by ferry. No visitor to Singapore should miss this trip.

At Hong Kong, to compensate for the lack of junks, there is a fine display of models of them at the Ocean Terminal. They must be the finest of their type to be seen anywhere in the world and are a credit to Chinese craftsmanship. These models are only partially planked, so that the internal construction is fully exposed. With such faithful reproduction of the Chinese shipwrights' craftsmanship they are complementary to the magnificent literary work and drawings* of George Worcester and his wife, so enabling us to appreciate more fully both Chinese boat and boatman.

Sail and Sweep in China, H.M. Stationery Office, London, 1966.
The Floating Population in China, Vetch & Lee Ltd., Hong Kong, 1970.
The Junks and Sampans of the Yangtze, Naval Institute Press, Annapolis, Maine, 1971.

Praus of Indonesia

To be in Indonesia is like returning to another age, so alive is commercial sail. Perhaps the only other comparable places are the west coast of India and the Brahmaputra-Ganges Delta in East Pakistan where the wind continues to be the main motive force for water transport.

Throughout Indonesia praus abound in such a great number of varying types that a new discovery might be made almost every day, so little is known about them. Throughout the Java Sea and Banda Sea to beyond Ceram and the Aru Islands, these are the home waters of the prau. Their trade, like that of the dhows, is more or less dependent upon the monsoonal changes. Most predominant in the fleet are the descendants of the Bugis praus from Sulawesi, the main island of what was formerly the Celebes. Many such craft, called pinisis, are now owned elsewhere — in Java and Sumatra — and, indeed, are even built there. Another and altogether different type of prau is that from the island of Madura across the strait from Surabaya.

I was in Indonesia during August 1978 and found both Tanjung Priok (Jakarta) and Tanjung Perak (Surabaya) crowded with pinisis and many other types of praus. Ujung Pandang, formerly known as Makassar, was most disappointing though, with very few trading praus in the harbour. This was probably because they were elsewhere awaiting the monsoonal change to bring them east. But what a pleasant surprise it was to encounter so many beautiful fishing praus there! These I chased in canoes fitted with bamboo outriggers and, most incongruously, an outboard engine.

Praus possess a number of peculiarities all of their own. First of all there is the manner in which they are constructed with their timbers dowelled together instead of being nailed or bolted. The most outstanding feature though is the tripod and bipod masting which, in the smaller craft, is of bamboo. Split bamboo and palm fronds also provide shelter for the crew and cargo in many of the praus. Then there is that extraordinary steering system comprised of quarter-rudders. Sails vary from those more typical of the European ketch to triangular and rectangular ones

that quite obviously originated when sails were made of matting from local fibre.

Only a few years ago permission to photograph the praus at Jakarta's Tanjung Priok was not readily granted but now, for a fee, entry to the prau berths adjacent to Pasar Ikan (the fish market) gives one the freedom to use a camera without any restriction or fear of having film confiscated. In contrast, at Tanjung Perak, photography is prohibited. This is because Surabaya is a naval port and, most unfortunately, the dockyard is close to the prau area.

At Ujung Pandang I saw cargoes of rattan and kapok, and praus loaded with soft drinks inward bound and 'empties' outward bound. Sulawesi could be a photographer's paradise. All the photogenic qualities are there, and much more, but I found mobs of undisciplined children a real problem. They took great delight in being an annoyance and there was no way to be rid of them. Suppressed in one direction, more would appear from elsewhere. Just one yell from a lone urchin would bring a mob upon me like a pack of orang utans, spelling an end to any photography I had in mind. So it was at Pare Pare, and the attitude of those youngsters is clearly seen in some of the photographs I purposely took to avoid a complete breakdown of a working relationship. If only they would find some other outlet for their exuberance, I thought!

In 1979 I revisited Indonesia and discovered at Jakarta's Kali Baru a harbour crowded with lateen-rigged Madura trading praus. Among them were some of the older type golekans of bifid construction and with heavily decorated transoms at both bow and stern. These praus carried great pick-like wooden anchors weighted at the ring end of the shank. One of them however, more privileged than the rest, possessed an iron anchor with a stock obviously of local manufacture.

One of my photographs shows two golekans discharging poles and logs and another is of a decorated bow transom with the upturned keel extension breaking water. There is a similar projection at the stern. Where else is it possible to see such vessels!

Praus at Sunda Kelapa, Jakarta (Indonesia 1978). *Right*, a juvenile confrontation, Pare Pare (Sulawesi 1978)

53

A prau pinisi at Sunda Kelapa (Jakarta 1978). *Below*, a fishing prau off Ujung Pandang, Sulawesi (1978). *Right*, laden with fish traps, the prau *Cahaya Galesong* (Ujung Pandang 1978)

Golekans unloading logs and poles at Kali Baru (Jakarta 1979) and *below*, an Indonesian golekan with a bifid stem and decorated fore transom (Kali Baru, Jakarta 1979). *Right*, a Madura leti-leti approaching Semarang (Indonesia 1979)

The Maori Canoe

Sir Bernard Freyberg VC, on the Waipa River (Ngaruawahia 1947)

ALTHOUGH this is essentially a biographical sketch of my life interest in photographing sail, the canoe does, and already has, come into the picture. So there is no reason why the Maori canoe should not be made welcome. After all, it did make voyages under sail on our coast.

Rarely does the opportunity arise for photographs to be taken of a Maori war canoe afloat as today the waka taua is a museum piece. Only those examples housed at Turangawaewae on the Waikato River and that at Waitangi in the Bay of Islands have been used in recent years, not to settle tribal differences but for ceremonial purposes. I photographed *Te Winika* on the Waipa River in 1947 when it conveyed the Governor General, Sir Bernard Freyberg, VC, to Turangawaewae for the lifting of tapu from the pa. This followed the return of members of the Maori Battalion from battle during World War II. Sir Bernard had been their commander and only he could lift the tapu that had been imposed during the absence of men overseas.

The prow (tauihu) of *Te Winika* is a fine example of Maori carving, with complete perforation of the wood. Projecting wands (ihi ihi) in early European times terminated with the puhi made from pigeon feathers. With the bird now protected these can no longer be used.

A war canoe of more recent times is the *Nga Toki Matawhaora*, constructed to take part in New Zealand's centennial celebrations at the Bay of Islands in 1940. Because of the country's involvement in World War II the canoe went into retirement without any ceremony taking place. The 117 foot craft was constructed from kauri trees felled in the Puketi forest. The bow and stern sections were adzed from one trunk, the centre from another, while the topstrakes came from a third tree. The photographs of the canoe and its crew were taken at Waitangi when Her Majesty Queen Elizabeth II and the Duke of Edinburgh visited New Zealand in 1974.

Small dugout canoes were in general use throughout New Zealand when European settlement first took place but, apart from being raced at the Ngaruawahia regatta each year, they are now rarely seen afloat. The *Lady Buck*, photographed on the Waikato River, was named after the wife of the late Sir Peter Buck, the noted Maori ethnologist. The decorated wale is more Pakeha than Maori in concept.

One might wonder where all the old canoes have disappeared to. During the 1860s they were still to be seen at Auckland's Mechanics Bay at the foot of Constitution Hill. Although small, some of these canoes possessed carved prows. Larger war canoes on the Manukau were destroyed as a punitive measure during the Maori Wars. They could easily have been placed in custody, but in an act of thoughtless vindictiveness their firing was demanded.

My memories of canoes can go back only to 1925 when I arrived in New Zealand as a boy. At that time small canoes were still in use on the Waikato, as they probably were on the Wanganui and elsewhere. I can remember one chained to the riverbank near Orakei Korako on the Waikato in 1937.

Although Ngaruawahia has been the venue for most of my canoe photography in New Zealand I have found that at nearby Turangawaewae a camera is looked upon with suspicion. The folk at the pa there almost go into a haka at the mere sight of a photographer!

Paddling for Turangawaewae (Waikato River 1971) and
below, the prow of *Te Winika* (Waipa River, Ngaruawahia
1947)

Lady Buck on the Waikato (Ngaruawahia 1971). *Below, Nga Toki Matawhaora* at Waitangi (1973)

The carved prow of *Nga Toki Matawhaora* and *below, Nga Toki Matawhaora's* paddlers (Waitangi 1973)

61

The New Zealand Scow

Some of my first photographic subjects were scows, and I came on the scene just in time to see the last of them working under sail. It was also my good fortune to make two trips to Omokoroa in the big logging scow *Rangi*, and a shorter one in the *Kitty Fraser* to Whangateau for a load of sand. Both scows were typical of their class and came from wellknown builders. The schooner-rigged *Rangi* was launched from Niccol's Auckland yard in 1905 and the ketch-rigged *Kitty Fraser* from Darroch's Big Omaha yard in 1911. These two scows were never engined and carried their gaff topsails right to the last.

My first voyage in the *Rangi* was a rare experience and proved to me that a large scow was quite as seaworthy as any other wooden sailing vessel. Auckland was cleared under ideal conditions but off Mercury Bay the next morning it was obvious that the weather had begun to deteriorate with a swell coming in from the nor'east. As the wind increased in strength the *Rangi* careered down the coast at the rate of knots, leaving behind her an incredible white wake. As the wind backed more northerly we ran wing and wing, with the seas beginning to show breaking crests.

Nearing the Tauranga entrance what an amazing sight ahead with a seething white line of breakers extending out from the spit off Matakana Island. Sail was shortened before we entered the maelstrom and I stationed myself amidships for some action. Above the roar of the surf I heard Captain Petersen call out to me. I believe he must have had fears for my safety, as at that moment a sea broke over the starboard rail and swirled about my feet. I got my picture but on turning to go aft there was an enormous sea about to give us a lift in on its crest, and all too soon the *Rangi* was in smooth water and making for an anchorage inside Matakana. Even now that surf roars in my ears. . .

In taking the photograph of the *Rangi's* lee rail awash while homeward bound the precaution was taken of tying a rope round my waist with Captain Petersen hanging on to its end. The deck under the logs would have then been awash right to the centreboard casings and at times water was swirling about the poop deck. To ease the scow we hove to off Colville and the fores'l was reefed.

The picture of the *Rangi* drying sails in Freemans Bay is now of some historic value. Not only have the logging scows vanished but the mills to which they brought the logs have also disappeared.

I took the photograph by going out on the floating logs. Leyland & O'Brien's mill was to the east of Parker Lamb's and then there was the Kauri Timber Company whose logs were rafted from the coast by the paddle tug *Lyttelton*. For me this was the most interesting part of the Auckland waterfront, with Niccol's shipyard adjacent to the KTC mill.

Flanking the west of Freemans Bay was Julian's Wall, where the sand and shingle scows discharged. The *Lyttelton* was also tied up there when there was no work for her. The scows used their own gear for discharging although I remember seeing the *Pahiki* unloading her shingle in barrels lifted out by a horse on the end of a whip.

The scow *Kitty Fraser* on the Waitemata (Auckland 1932)

The scow *Rangi* hemmed in by logs at Auckland's Freemans Bay (1936)

Auckland's skyline over the centreboard cases of the *Rangi* as the scow sails out of the Waitemata for Omokoroa (1934). *Below*, off Rangitoto beacon with little weight in the wind

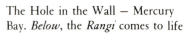
The Hole in the Wall — Mercury Bay. *Below*, the *Rangi* comes to life

In the Bay of Plenty with a bone in her teeth. *Right*, a winter squall (1936)

As the wind increases the sea becomes rougher and the jib-tops'l is taken in (1934)

Breakers ahead off Matakana
Island. The fore gaff-tops'l is taken
in and *right* in the maelstrom of
broken water a sea comes aboard.
Below, at anchor under the lee of
Matakana

At Omokoroa. Loading rimu logs

At sea again, master, cook and boy
all work together. The *Rangi*
carried a crew of five including
the master. *Below*, Harold
Helgeson at the wheel

73

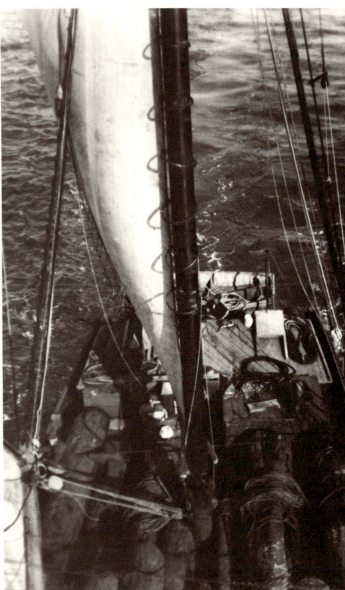

A spanking westerly puts the scow's lee rail down. Later the boy at the wheel was thrown to the deck when the pressure on the rudder became too much for him to manage. *Above*, Captain Petersen holds the *Rangi* on her course

Reefing the fores'l and *below* making for the Needles off Colville

Back in the Waitemata. Off Devonport with logs from Puriri (1933) and *below*, end of the voyage (Freemans Bay, Auckland 1937)

The Leyland O'Brien mill, Auckland, with kauri logs in the boom and the *Rangi* at her moorings (1935). *Below*, the remains of the *Rangi* (Wade River, Hauraki Gulf 1937)

Square Rig

URING the 1930s a number of deep-water square-rigged sailing ships made voyages to New Zealand with guano from the Seychelles Islands. They were among the last of the square-riggers still in commission, and I always welcomed their visits for the rare opportunity they afforded for photographing such vessels, hopefully under sail. The fact that these arrivals took place during our mid-summer did not necessarily mean that they would coincide with good weather. So often these barques entered or left port during heavy rain or under a leaden sky but, rain or sunshine, I was ever on the lookout for sail and my patience oft-times resulted in photographs well worth the chase.

The first big sailing vessel I ever set eyes on was the old *Rewa* which during my school years was laid up in the upper reaches of the Waitemata. Many of my own age would remember that four-masted barque and maybe the Down-Easter *Guy C. Goss* too. She was the first square-rigged sailing ship that I saw actually in commission, but soon after her arrival at Auckland in 1926 the owners were in financial difficulties and her sea career came to an abrupt end with a writ nailed to the mainmast. But photography had not entered my life at that time and it was not until 1931 that I was able to take my first picture of a sailing ship — with a cheap box camera. It was of the *Grace Harwar*, a true full-rigged ship and the one in which Alan Villiers rounded the Horn in 1929 to form the basis of his book *By Way of Cape Horn*.

A sailing ship can be photographed as often as you like and yet each occasion will produce a completely different picture. A good example of this is illustrated here with photographs of the barque *Pamir* taken under sail on four different occasions, first when inward bound at Auckland in 1938 while under the flag of Finland; outward bound from Wellington in 1946; and inward and outward at Auckland in 1948 while under the New Zealand flag. Such photographic work was not often achieved without the assistance given by numerous good friends in the shipping world, but always it was the weather that meant so much. A sailing ship must have wind, and I can remember days of anxious waiting for it to come from the right quarter before the *Pamir* could sail.

It has been my good fortune to have the opportunity to photograph some of the finest examples of square-rigged sailing ships that were ever built in the famed European shipyards at the turn of the century. The *Grace Harwar*, sole representative from Britain, was Clyde-built by W. Hamilton & Company at Glasgow in 1889. Rickmers of Bremerhaven is represented by the *Winterhude* of 1898, bald-headed by the time I photographed her in 1933. The *Penang* also came from the Rickmers' yard, in 1905. These three vessels were all flush-decked amidships and consequently, when deeply laden, were prone to being swept from end to end by seas breaking over the rail. The *Passat*, *Pamir* and *Kommodore Johnsen* were built with a 'midship 'island' which not only provided a deck not so likely to be swept by unruly seas but also made it possible to steer from amidships. Then too there was the advantage of having accommodation for both officers and seamen within the 'islands', so doing away with quarters in the forecastle and under the poop.

The 'midship structure was very popular with German shipowners and it can be seen in my photographs of the four-masted barques. Both the *Pamir* and the *Passat* were built by Blohm & Voss at Hamburg for F. Laeisz, the *Pamir* in 1905 and the *Passat* in 1911. Krupps of Kiel built the *Kommodore Johnsen* as the *Magdalene Vinnen* in 1921. She first came to Auckland in 1933 when owned by F. A. Vinnen and later under the North German Lloyd flag. She is now the Russian training ship *Sedov*.

With guano from the Seychelles the ship *Grace Harwar*
arrives at Auckland (1932)

The German barque *Magdalene Vinnen* afloat and in
Calliope Dock, Devonport (Auckland 1934)

The barque *Passat* in the Hauraki Gulf outward bound for
the Spencer Gulf (1933)

The *Passat* was built for the Laeisz
Line of Hamburg. *Right*, main
deck, barque *Winterhude* (Hauraki
Gulf 1933)

Bound for Wallaroo under the flag of Gustav Erikson.
Right, going aloft to loosen gaskets, barque
Winterhude (Hauraki Gulf 1933)

The barque *Penang* of Finland
making for Auckland ... from
alongside ... fores'l and tops'ls,
(1938)

Aboard the *Penang*; about to take
in sail, at the main shrouds
and furling the mains'l.

The Finnish barque *Pamir*
approaching Auckland with a
cargo of guano from the Seychelles
(1938)

Under the New Zealand flag the *Pamir*, bound for Vancouver, is escorted out of Port Nicholson by the *Terawhiti* (1946) and *below*, in the *Pamir's* rigging (Hauraki Gulf 1938)

The *Pamir* gets under way (Wellington 1946)

Pamir nearing the end of her voyage from Antwerp to Auckland. *Right*, in Rangitoto Channel and showing her wake to the *William C. Daldy* (1948)

Early morning on the Waitemata. *Below*, in tow of the *William C. Daldy* (Auckland to Wellington 1948)

Backs are bent to a halliard winch
and muscles strain as sail is set

The mizzen mast and *right*, farewell *Pamir* (Hauraki Gulf 1948)

Sail in the Mediterranean

IN A PORT AREA one can so easily run foul of the law, as I discovered at Naples in 1939 while photographing on a quay crowded with beautiful Italian sailing ships. I had taken but three pictures when an eagle-eyed officer of the carabinieri spotted me. 'No! No!' argued my guide on my behalf, 'He hasn't taken any photos, he is only making notes.' This despite the fact that I had the camera in my hand and obviously in use and the notes were nothing more than the names of two of the sailing vessels. The outcome was that no more photographs could be taken but I was allowed to leave with the three already on the film and which I now consider to be among the most valuable pictures in my collection. Few if any of these sailing ships survived the war that was so soon to make this quay enemy territory.

For the record, the brigantine *San Francesco di Paola D* of Trapani was built as the *Maria Luisa Tonetti* at Viareggio in 1914. Astern of her was the barquentine *Cristina* of Genoa, built at Savona as the *Elenora* in 1902. She sailed under that name until 1937 when she was renamed *Luisa Rosa*, finally changing to *Cristina* a year later. Further along the quay was a host of other sailing vessels, all of which must for ever remain unidentified. In examining the photographs we obtain a glimpse of beautifully-turned wooden stanchions supporting the *Cristina's* fo'castle rail and the heavy wooden stock of the starboard anchor. Rigging is secured with deadeyes and lanyards, and there is a wooden water cask on board the brigantine. These are ships from a bygone era.

In the eastern Mediterranean the Levant staysail schooner is a development of more recent years. Those seen at Port Said in 1959 were Israeli vessels. Although photographed from different levels, by a stroke of good luck the tanker *Naess Venturer* forms a continuous related background. This type of schooner appears to be an adaptation of the caique which once traded in Greek waters and to Cyprus, Lebanon, Israel and along the coast right through Egypt to Libya. Notable for their tall raking pole masts and exceptionally long steep bowsprits, the caiques were also staysail-schooner rigged. To my lasting regret I never had the opportunity to photograph any of these vessels, and now I believe they are all gone. Present-day caiques are but a shadow of those that sailed before World War II.

One of the joys of sea travel is the meeting of other ships, but because passenger liners are now such a rarity on the old ocean routes such pleasures are denied to practically all but those who take up a sea career — and even their chance of falling in with a sailing ship is rather remote. It was far different back in the northern spring of 1939. Westbound through the Mediterranean in the *Orion* we passed two brigantines on approaching the Strait of Messina and another in the Bay of Naples the following morning. Then came the forest of masts and spars within the port of Naples itself. Some days later, while passing through the Strait of Gibraltar, we overtook a schooner bucking into head seas as she sailed close-hauled out into the Atlantic.

Italian sail, Naples. The *San Francesco di Paola D* of Trapani (1939)

The *Cristina* of Genoa astern of the
San Francesco di Paola D, opposite
and *right*, in close-up (1939). *Below*,
Levant schooners at Port Said
(1959)

Barges

I FIRST ENCOUNTERED the English sailing barge in 1939 on the Thames and Medway Rivers and in later years on the Orwell and Blackwater. The photograph taken at Rochester illustrates a typical situation that arises through lack of wind, with a barge being poled as its sails hang limp and useless. During the summer of 1939 I also haunted the Thames at Woolwich and through sheer determination secured one worthwhile shot from the free ferry. Barges, one after the other, were passing down river on the tide and I repeatedly crossed and recrossed on the ferry in the hope of catching one in midstream. At last I was rewarded with this one photograph, so different from anything that I had ever anticipated. By the white cross on her tops'l the barge can be identified as belonging to H. & W. Paul & Co. of Ipswich.

Although generally referred to as Thames barges these craft also came from other rivers such as the Medway and Orwell. Some traded well beyond these south-eastern estuaries of England and sailed across the North Sea to Belgium and Holland and down channel to the West Country, the Bristol Channel and Irish ports. Barges were the workhorses of the London River, distributing cargoes direct from liners in the docks and transporting bricks, cement, grain, flour, fertiliser and other bulk cargoes. Rarely did a barge resort to the use of auxiliary power until competition forced it to.

The *Veronica* was photographed on the Medway during the 1959 Medway Barge Race. She was built at East Greenwich in 1906 for Essex owners and was later purchased by F. T. Everard & Sons. Oft-times she was Champion barge of both Thames and Medway races in the same year. Barges like her were kept as yachts and carried sails not customarily used in working craft. The races were divided into two classes, one for barges with bowsprits and another called the Staysail Class. *Sara, Veronica* and *Sirdar* were in the Bowsprit Class.

The *Sara* was another Everard barge and was built at Conyer in 1902. *Sirdar*, the oldest of the trio, was built at Ipswich in 1898, her owners being the London & Rochester Trading Co. In the races these barges were crewed by five hands as well as the master. The year 1959 was the occasion of the fifty-first Medway Race and some real veterans competed. *Millie* was the oldest, dating back to 1892, when she was built at Brightlingsea. Then there was the *Maid of Connaught*, built at Greenwich in 1899. Eastwood's *Westmoreland* from Conyer in 1900, the *Memory* that had been built at Harwich in 1904 was looking spick and span following her restoration by the Sailing Barge Preservation Society, and also the *Dreadnought* of 1907 from Sittingbourne.

The course for the Thames race was forty-eight miles from Lower Hope Point to North Oaze Buoy and back to Gravesend. The Medway course started from Gillingham and followed round the West Oaze Buoy and back. In 1978, with a race scheduled to be run out of the Orwell, I found Pin Mill a grand place for mudlarking. There was a sizable fleet of barges assembled on the river preparing for the big day and I had plenty of time for photography between tides. But there were some anxious moments when, standing in one place for too long, I found myself sinking deeper and deeper in the mud until it was almost impossible to extricate myself. On the morning of the race I had already done a hard day's work long before breakfast.

The comparatively few sailing barges — some fifty or so — that remain afloat are mostly privately owned as yachts or are employed in charter work. To own one can be a costly business with perhaps £30,000 for its purchase in sailing condition. Just to re-rig one would cost something like £2,000 using existing masts and spars.

As an indication of the escalation of prices, in 1891 the cost of making an 85 square yard topsail and a 245½ square yard mainsail for a sprits'l barge was £30 19s 10½d. In 1976 similar sails would possibly have cost about £1,500.

The Medway at Chatham (1939) and *below*, out on the tide.
Woolwich Reach (River Thames 1939)

Waiting for orders, Rochester (1939). *Below*, Medway Barge
Race, *Sara* leads *Veronica* and *Sirdar*, and *right*, *Veronica*
close hauled on the starboard tack (1959)

Westmoreland and *Millie* on the Medway and *left*, the *Dreadnought* of London in the Thames estuary (1959). *Right, Ironsides* off Harwich (1978)

Phoenician (North Sea 1978) and
below, *Xylonite* in the Medusa
Channel off Harwich (1978).
Right, off the Naze from *Atalanta*
(1978)

Ebb tide at Pin Mill and *right*, on the River Orwell (Suffolk 1978)

112

Seascapes

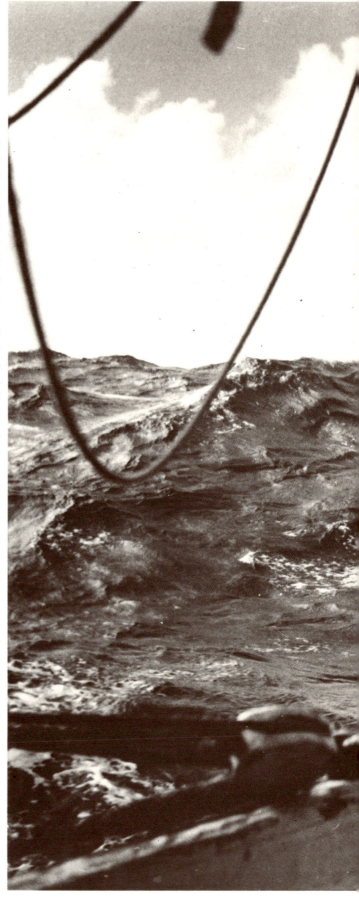

Even though the sailing ship has taken precedence over all else in my photography not always has it been possible to compose an acceptable seascape because of poor weather conditions. At such times there is no alternative but to create something from the negatives by using one's skill in the darkroom.

Some purposely-made seascapes are the result of having taken advantage of sea and cloud from the deck of a sailing vessel and making use of rigging, such as deadeyes and lanyards, for added interest.

The *Huia* was ideal for this as the photographs taken aboard her in the Pacific show. In one the schooner has taken a lurch to port, sending an expanse of broken water out from the hull. This conveys the required impression of movement which, of course, there actually was. In another shot taken from a similar position aboard the *Huia* the focal point is more distant and the clouds, soaring up from the horizon, hold one's interest beyond the vessel herself.

With the *Gloria* entering Wellington Harbour conditions were absolutely atrocious. During the night it blew a hard 'southerly buster' with driving rain. Arrangements had been made to join a launch laid on for the news media in the early hours, and when we left the Queens Wharf rain was still coming down in torrents. Dawn was just breaking as we picked out the Colombian training ship in the murk off Barretts Reef and although the lighting was extremely poor the rain had started to ease. Plunging into those seas would have made photography impossible anyway but, on turning to run in, conditions became more comfortable.

The *Gloria* had already taken in her sails and, under power, got ahead of us with no photographs having been taken. Then, looking aft, I saw a monstrous wall of water coming up on us direct from Cook Strait. 'Look at this, Jack!' I yelled out to my companion.* 'Hold on until it passes and get a low-angle shot of her hull down!' We each managed to make one exposure. Jack was using high-speed colour and my black-and-white film rating was little better.

*E. J. Churchouse, now Curator of the Wellington Maritime Museum.

From the schooner *Huia* (Auckland to Suva 1951)

But the lighting sufficed on the widest of apertures with the use of just sufficient shutter-speed to eliminate any blurring movement. Jack's transparency took a first award in the New Zealand Ship & Marine Society's 1971 Photo Contest and we were both happy.

In retrospect I would liked to have taken my picture from a position some distance to port, as that would have given a clear gap between the Seatoun Heights and the *Gloria* as well as making it possible to take greater advantage of the larger wave mass in that direction. Conditions over there however might have made photography more difficult, especially with what would have been a sharper angle of approach. So let us be content with what we have, remembering that this was where the *Wahine* inter-Island passenger ferry had so tragically foundered two years earlier, with the loss of over fifty lives.

Some of my photographs, and that of the *Gloria* was one, were obtained only through travelling long distances, but others came about because I habitually carried a camera to and from work as my route was by way of the waterfront. Leave the camera behind and, sure enough, I would miss out on something. The *Cap Pilar* is a pre-work study and the *A'oniu* is the result of an after-work diversion. This vessel, built of Vanikoro kauri at Suva, was photographed at Auckland's Okahu Bay in 1955. She had previously visited the Waitemata in 1952 for the fitting of a new hardwood keel after receiving structural damage on a Tongan reef. The evening cloud formation reflecting in the mud makes this picture. As an auxiliary ketch, the *A'oniu* was not a good-looking craft and without that beautiful lighting a photograph would not have been considered worth while.

Clouds are again the predominant feature in the early morning picture of the *Cap Pilar*. This barquentine was an ex-Grand Banks fisherman out of St Malo in France, and having made her last voyage in that capacity had been purchased by an Englishman, Adrian Seligman, for a world cruise. My photograph was taken in 1937 as the vessel entered the Waitemata Harbour. Over twenty years later I again met up with the *Cap Pilar* at Wivenhoe in Essex; a sorry sight, lying derelict with the muddy waters of the Colne flowing through her rotted timbers. I had gone to Wivenhoe to see where the Melanesian Mission's *Southern Cross* had been built back in 1891, not realising that nearby lay the remains of an old acquaintance.

The estuaries of Suffolk and Essex have provided me with many a pleasurable occasion. Even though the sailing craft have mostly gone their old haunts remain. I found a rare link with the past at Snape on the Alde River and another at Woodbridge on the Deben. Then, at Ramsholt, sail enthusiast Robert Simper introduced me to his *Atalanta*, an old pilot cutter from across the North Sea. Under gaff rig I followed a barge race out of the Orwell in this craft. Some years previously, at Maldon on the Blackwater, I came across the remnants of a one-time fleet of Essex oyster dredgers lying high and dry on the same muddy river bank that was the home of so many of these craft at the turn of the century.

Deadeyes and lanyards (*left*) and
the loss of the *Huia*, Komekame
Reef, New Caledonia (1951)

117

The *Gloria* entering Port
Nicholson (1970)

The southseaman *Tiare Taporo* (Hauraki Gulf 1962). *Below*, beached for repairs. The Tongan ketch *A'oniu* (Okahu Bay, Auckland 1955)

An early morning arrival. The barquentine *Cap Pilar* sails
into the Waitemata (1937) and *right*, a dying ship; the
derelict *Cap Pilar* at Wivenhoe (River Colne 1959)

From the fore crosstrees, scow *Rangi* (off Colville 1936).
Right, *Klaraborg* in the Bay of Plenty (1978)

Oyster smacks at Maldon, Essex (1967). *Right* the Brixham trawler *Arthur Rogers* at Auckland (1953)

Maldon on the Blackwater (1967)

Restoration and Reconstruction

WHEN a nautically-minded friend visited Britain for the first time it did not take him long to gravitate to the maritime museums and exhibition ships, which included the *Cutty Sark* at Greenwich and the *Victory* at Portsmouth. This friend returned to his New Zealand home very disappointed because he had not been able to see the stern galleries of the famous ship of the line as her stern had been under repair and behind scaffolding. So here are the stern galleries, Rod, as I saw them back in '59. It was I who was then disappointed because at that time the bows were under repair and in no condition to face a camera.

As might be expected, very little of *Victory's* original timber has survived the ravages of beetle and decay. Major restoration-work over the years has given us almost a new ship. Originally the stern consisted of a tier of open walkways. Late in the eighteenth century these were dispensed with in the big men o'war in order to give greater strength to their hulls, and at Trafalgar the open stern walks of the *Victory* had disappeared. The galleries in my photograph show the stern as it was in 1805.

A ship that has outlived the purpose for which she was built is rather saddening, especially if she is converted to a show boat. The life has gone out of her. In a final gasp for survival though, she might show the flag out of San Diego or stir someone's imagination in Picton with an appeal for help. Yet sometimes a ship does gain new life with restoration and one of them is the whaler *Charles W. Morgan* at Mystic, Connecticut. When I photographed this barque in 1951 sea-cadets from not far distant Weatherly were receiving some practical training in the handling of sail. Since then the *Morgan* has become even more alive by being refloated. And what a beautiful haven Mystic is for oldtimers to retire in.

The exhibition ship of Britain is the *Cutty Sark*, although she now has a serious competitor for popularity in the steamship *Great Britain* at Bristol. Although, like the *Cutty Sark*, the *Great Britain* spent part of her career on the Australian run, the two cannot really be compared. I would however prefer to see the hold of the *Cutty Sark* stowed with chests of tea rather than with rows of figureheads.

But what an advantage it is for the clipper to be in a dock, so making it possible for her underwater lines to be fully appreciated and compared with those of the latter-day steel barque *Pamir*. The differences of hull form are immediately apparent. The clipper ship was of course built to carry specialised cargoes in as short a time as possible under sail, whereas barques like the *Pamir* were designed to haul large bulk cargoes economically. Even though good passages were often made by them, speed was secondary to capacity.

Not so well known for their restoration are the *barques* (barges) *de Lac Leman*. In the early 1900s Lake Geneva (Lac Leman) was dotted with these lateen-sailed craft which were employed in much the same manner as were the scows in North America and New Zealand, carrying their cargo above deck; but, being lateeners, the Swiss vessels were more typical of those in the Mediterranean.

The *barque de Lac Leman* was constructed with the deck winged out over the sides of the hull, so allowing a larger cargo to be carried. The vessel could also be punted from these wings should the water be shallow enough. Normally twin lateen sails and a staysail were set. Only two of these *barques* are now afloat on Lake Geneva, the *Neptune* at Geneva and the *Vaudoise* at Lausanne. I first came across the latter craft in 1959, then again in 1978. During the intervening years the hull had gradually deteriorated despite attempts to preserve it by sheathing the planking with polyester. This did not prevent rot from setting in, and it had been found necessary to carry out extensive reconstruction. The lesson must be learned from Mystic Seaport that the most satisfactory way to preserve a wooden hull is to put back similar materials to those that were originally used. It is good to know that there is now another of these old *barques*, the *Neptune*, running trips out on the lake from Geneva. She was built in 1904.

The clipper ship *Cutty Sark* (Greenwich 1959)

There are many other ships all over the world that have been restored in varying degree, and perhaps the most wonderful of all is the *Vasa* at Stockholm. It is difficult to mention one and not another because so many are important in their own right; and there is every likelihood that even greater feats of restoration will eventuate with the development of underwater technology.

Bows of the British composite-built clipper *Cutty Sark* (Greenwich 1959) and the German-built steel nitrate carrier *Pamir* (Auckland 1938)

Stern galleries of the *Victory* (Portsmouth 1959)

Barque de Lac Leman. The *Vaudoise* at Lausanne (1959) and
under repair (1978)

The whaleship *Charles W. Morgan* at Mystic, Connecticut and looking for a berth! (Mystic 1967)

The barque *Viking* and schooner *Valborg* (Gothenburg 1978)

The Gloucester fishing schooner
W. A. Dunton (Mystic 1967) and
The Gloucesterman *Henrietta* at
Hobart (1939)

Australian Ketches

WHEN I passed through Hobart in 1939 a few of the ketches that at one time had been such a feature of the port were tied up in the old Victoria and Constitution Docks. Some of them still set the old fashioned jackyard topsails.

The *Foam* and *Tayanna* provided the reflections in my Hobart photographs and several other ketches were there too, among them the *Margaret Twaits*, *Enterprise* and *Evaleeta*. The *Evaleeta* was a beauty, built at Port Cygnet on the Huon River in 1923. During World War II she was one of the small craft requisitioned for service in the Pacific Islands, and so it was that I again met up with this lovely vessel when I was at Noumea in 1951. She was then trading out of that port, but her career came to a close some time later when she sank at her moorings in the Mary River, Queensland.

The Tasmanian ketches were hard to match, not only for their good looks but also for their seaworthiness. They were built to operate in some of the most treacherous coastal waters known, in the Bass Strait and the Tasman Sea on the east coast of Tasmania. Consequently a hull was evolved which gave all that could be desired under extremely trying conditions. Their flush decks were remarkably free of clutter so that there was little to be lost overboard during rough weather. In some of the vessels, besides the main cabin aft, there was accommodation for the crew in the forecastle, together with the galley, below deck. This was the arrangement with the *Evaleeta* as I saw it in New Caledonia.

The ketches were often fitted with spike bowsprits but the *Evaleeta* and the *Miena* which came to New Zealand had separate sprit and jib-boom. The *Miena* arrived at Auckland from Port Arthur in 1938 after sailing right through a terrific storm that kept the transtasman passenger liner *Wanganella* hove to. The little ketch did get quite a dusting though and, besides having her tiller damaged, lost two jibs. But then the *Wanganella* did not come through this midwinter storm unscathed either, so that the seagoing capabilities of the Tasmanian ketch had been well proven. After some years sailing out of Auckland she joined other small craft for war service in the Pacific.

Then, in 1962, the *Miena* sank at her moorings at Tulagi and, although she was raised and beached, was eventually broken up.

I think a greater number of Australian sailing vessels crossed the Tasman to go on New Zealand registry than did New Zealand craft going the opposite way. This despite the fact that the dominion was a noted shipbuilding country. Probably it was all a matter of convenience that decided where or when a sale was to be made. Not always was the right type of vessel available immediately it was required by a New Zealand owner, perhaps because of a loss or an unexpected increase in trade. So a prospective buyer was often forced to go across the Tasman to make a purchase.

In Auckland during the 1930s there were two Australian-built ketches that, despite their age, were not written off until the end of the war. The oldest was the *Huon Belle*, and the name gives the clue to her origin: she was built away back in 1864 at Port Cygnet on Tasmania's Huon River. During her first year or two this ketch was employed carrying logs from the Huon River to Hobart but after crossing the Tasman with a load of hardwood for Wanganui in 1867 she came under New Zealand ownership, with Dunedin and then Lyttelton as her home port. In 1896 J. J. Craig of Auckland acquired the *Huon Belle* and for years she carried cement between Whangarei and Auckland. As a ketch the vessel originally had topmasts from which jack-yard topsails were set. An older vessel, the *Huon Chief*, built in 1849, was similar to the *Huon Belle*, and a *Huon Pine* was of even earlier vintage.

The second ketch remembered was the *Will Watch*, but she was from New South Wales, having been built at Blackwall in 1895. In New Zealand she carried numerous coal cargoes from Whangarei to Auckland and it was on one such trip that I photographed her on the Waitemata in 1935. Normally the hull was painted black — appropriate enough for coal cargoes — but before I took the photograph the *Will Watch* had been converted to carry scientists on expeditions to various islands off the northern coast and, to be more in keeping with such work, had been painted white. A most unusual feature of the ketch was the size of the mainsail when compared with the mizzen.

Hobart ketches. The *Foam* and *Taynna* (1939)

Hobart. The ketches *Foam, Taynna* and *Enterprise* (1939)
and *right*, the Hobart ketch *Evaleeta* (Noumea 1951)

The Tasmanian-built *Miena* on the slipway at Auckland (1938)

The *Huon Belle* in her seventieth
year (Auckland 1933) and the *Will
Watch* (Auckland 1935)

Baltic Traders

Occasionally an ex-Baltic trader has ventured to the South Seas and at Auckland provided a welcome change to the local waterfront scene. The *Fri* was one of them, and I photographed her in the Hauraki Gulf in 1972 before she ran foul of the French authorities by sailing into the nuclear testing zone off Mururoa Atoll. The ketch was built at Svendborg in Denmark in 1912 and was strengthened in the bows for work in the ice. When her career in the Baltic came to a close she was sold, in 1967, to a Californian sailing enthusiast. David Moodie, her present owner, then bought the *Fri* and under the Peace flag has visited New Zealand, the Russian port of Nakhodka, Hong Kong, and other exotic places too numerous to keep track of. After overhauling in Sri Lanka she crossed the Indian Ocean to the African continent and has since arrived in England.

In 1978, while passing through Sausalito on the shores of San Francisco bay, I spied among all the yachts the masts and spars of a topsail schooner. She was the *Lady Frei* from Aalborg, and in fine shape she was too. But to my astonishment a false clipper stem had been fitted bearing the figurehead of an American bald eagle. But that was not all, for projecting from over the bowsprit was a jib-boom, looking completely out of place. I felt that this lovely Baltic schooner had taken the 'oath of allegiance' to please her owner, but nothing could disguise the fact that this was not a true American. For ever she would be Scandinavian by nature, despite attempts to camouflage her true identity.

A real oldtimer is the *Klaraborg*, in which I made a trip on the New Zealand coast in 1978. She is well over a century old, having been built at Sjötorp on Lake Vanern, Sweden, in 1860. *Sveriges Skeppslista*, however, gives no date or place of construction. It does say though that she was built as the *Jesper* of *ek* and *feru* (oak and fir) and was rigged as a galleas. Owned in Vanersborg on Lake Vanern, the *Klaraborg* was registered at Gothenburg and to reach the sea she would have passed through the Gota Canal. In 1978 I visited Sweden and made a point of seeing members of the family who formerly owned this galleas. They spoke of her in most endearing terms as if she had been a member of the family. The photograph from the jib-boom was taken while the *Klaraborg* was off Gable End Foreland earlier in the year.

In Scandinavia I was in the home waters of Baltic sailing craft, and located a number of them in various ports. One was the immaculate schooner *Aron* of Svendborg, which was visiting Gothenburg, and another, the *Isefjord*, built at Frederikshavn in 1874, was seen running trips out of Copenhagen. In that city's Nyhavn Canal there is quite a varied collection of Baltic types. The clinker-built fishing cutter *Kastrup*; the ketches *Ariel*, *Bona* and *Mari*, and the schooner *Saga*, all in varying stages of restoration. This old dock area lined with warehouses, beer-halls and ship-chandlery premises recalls Copenhagen's salty past, as does the monumental wooden-stocked anchor bearing the date 1857.

Scandinavia has a wonderful maritime history of which the present-day Nordic generation is made well aware of through the beautiful museums and in the retrieval of centuries-old Viking ships, the *Vasa*, and sailing vessels of more recent times.

Fri under the flag of Peace (Hauraki Gulf 1972)

Danish-built – American-owned. The *Fri* in the Hauraki Gulf (1972)

The *Lady Frei* of Aalborg at
Sausalito, San Francicso Bay. A
false stern and trailboards
Americanise her (1978)

The Swedish ketch *Klaraborg*, her figurehead was carved in Fiji. 'Armstrong's Patent', weighing anchor in the *Klaraborg* (off Motutapu, Hauraki Gulf 1977). *Right, Klaraborg* off Gable End Foreland (1978)

The Danish schooner *Isefjord* at Copenhagen (1978) and *left*, the schooner *Aron* of Svendborg, which was built at Marstal in 1906 (Gothenburg 1978)

The lap-strake jagt *Kastrup* at Copenhagen (1978). *Below*, the Nyhavn Canal, Copenhagen. The anchor is dated 1857 (1978)

Sail-Training Ships

A SAIL-TRAINING SHIP invariably attracts a huge crowd of sightseers, and the arrival of the Argentinian *Libertad* at Sydney in 1970 to take part in Australia's Cook bicentennial celebrations turned out to be a spectacle equalled only by the magnificent fireworks display a few nights later. It was a glorious morning and an enthralling sight with all the 'fizz' boats closing in on the visiting ship in droves and creating a terrific din. Such diversions are not usually appreciated by the sailing-ship enthusiast, who considers power and sail incompatible; but this was a happy occasion, and the more the merrier!

With the *Esmeralda's* departure from Auckland in 1966 the situation was quite different, and I was able to hang on to the Chilean until she was well out in the Hauraki Gulf and clear of all the clutter of farewelling craft. What a pity that events in Chile have caused a union ban to be imposed on this vessel to prevent her entering a New Zealand port.

The arrival of the *Gloria* at Wellington in 1970 has already been referred to. Her departure was delayed by frustrating strike action by a section of harbour employees, and when at last the mooring lines were released it was getting late in the day. Worse still, as sail was being made, drizzle set in and it became so dark when the photographs were being taken that navigation lights had been switched on. As the Colombian barque disappeared into the murk in the direction of Cook Strait we watched young molly-mawks practising take-offs and landings, to make a very pleasant end to an otherwise disappointing day.

The large square-rigged training ships (barques, etc.) are employed almost exclusively for the training of naval cadets or, in some instances, those who intend taking up a career in their country's merchant navy. Alternatively there are small sailing vessels like those belonging to the British Sail Training Association which give young people who do not necessarily intend to become professional sailors the opportunity to live and work together as a group while gaining some practical knowledge of seamanship through the medium of sail.

In New Zealand there is an organisation that provides a service to the community similar to that of the British Sail Training Association. This was made possible by the gift of a training schooner by an Auckland industrial businessman, the late L. J. Fisher. The vessel, named *Spirit of Adventure*, is entirely the product of New Zealand expertise, designed by the Auckland naval architect John Brooke and built at the yard of Vos and Brijs at Auckland. She has a length of 105 feet overall, a beam of 22 feet and draught of 10 feet 6 inches.

The *Spirit* was launched in 1973 and has since been making something like twenty-five voyages a year with young trainees from all parts of the country. Although they are taught how to handle a boat and the rudimentary elements of navigation, the main purpose of the Trust is to develop confidence and initiative in the young people. There are opportunities however for adults to make short trips and to experience what is available for the younger ones. The photograph of the schooner was taken off Rakino Island in the Hauraki Gulf, a chance meeting when crossing from Coromandel to Okura in the *Ripple* and from one of the schooners own boats.

The Argentinian ship *Libertad* entering Port Jackson to partake in Australia's Cook bi-centennial celebrations (Sydney 1970)

Libertad (Port Jackson 1970), *below*, *Esmeralda* (Hauraki Gulf 1966). *Right*, *Gloria* of Columbia (Wellington 1970)

The *Spirit of Adventure* (Hauraki Gulf 1977 and 1979)

Spirit of Adventure in the Hauraki Gulf. The schooner's
training programme also extends to the southern centres of
New Zealand (1979)

Replicas

IN RECENT YEARS there has been a resurgence of interest in the restoration of old ships and the construction of replicas. Most widely known of the latter class are the *Bounty* (1960), the *Mayflower* (1957) and the *Bluenose* (1963). Not so publicised is the *Nonsuch*, which was built in 1968 for the Hudson Bay Company as a lifesize copy of their ketch that, three hundred years before, had sailed into Hudson Bay for the first cargo of beaver skins.

A project that failed to materialise was the proposal to build a replica of Cook's *Endeavour* and to sail her in the track of the great navigator's first voyage of discovery. This was to coincide with the bicentennial celebrations to be held in New Zealand and Australia in honour of Cook. When the scheme collapsed one New Zealander decided that he would build his own *Endeavour*, and in a matter of a few months Ralph Sewell, with a number of his friends, produced a twenty-two foot replica of the famous bark. While this was on the stocks Ralph's wife was busy working on the sails as well as performing her normal household tasks and looking after the children. This miniature *Endeavour* was a marvellous sea boat; she took part in various Cook celebrations throughout New Zealand and showed the flag in Australia. She is now housed in the Russell Museum at the Bay of Islands.

What the Australians did was a comparatively sorry affair. In Vancouver there had been built a little barque called the *Monte Cristo*. This was renamed *Endeavour II*, and she crossed the Pacific to take part in the re-enactment of Cook's landing at Botany Bay. In February 1971 this vessel left Brisbane for Auckland and successfully crossed the Tasman Sea, only to be caught on a lee shore after rounding North Cape and wrecked at the entrance to Parengarenga Harbour. My photograph of the unfortunate vessel was taken at Sydney after the ceremony in Botany Bay. As a backdrop is the then uncompleted Opera House, which is not too much of a distraction in the photograph since the hardwood piles take the eyes directly to our subject tied up at the wharf.

The *Ripple*, another little sailing vessel built by Ralph Sewell, represents the shallow-draught ketch of that name which plied on the Manukau Harbour earlier this century. The replica is a handy craft serving the dual purpose of yacht and private work-boat. As in the original *Ripple* a centreboard can be lowered whenever required. Accommodation is provided in the main cabin and in the forecastle. The hold can be converted to sleeping quarters or be put to any other use, making this the most practical of all replicas.

Now, surpassing all else, a *Bounty* has been built in New Zealand for overseas film interests. The Whangarei Engineering Company won the contract to construct this replica of Bligh's ship — in steel but sheathed with 1½ inch planking above the waterline. My photographs were taken in March this year (1979) during sea trials in Bream Bay. Although the original *Bounty* had a complement of forty-four the New Zealand replica was sailed on her trails by a crew of twenty, thirteen of whom were boys and young men who had received training in or were associated with the *Spirit of Adventure*. And how well the task was performed — with only one mock flogging, for the fun of it.

This new *Bounty* has a length on the waterline of 86 feet 10 inches and a beam of 24 feet 10 inches over the fenders. The draught is 12 feet 6 inches with fuel and fresh water aboard.

Masts and spars are of Columbian pine, and the sails, totalling 10,000 square feet, are made from Scottish flax by Ratsey & Lapthorn of Cowes. Eleven miles of rigging came from a Hull rope manufacturer; the stays and shrouds being of 4 inch, 6 inch and 8 inch manilla. Some of the standing rigging is served with wire to conform with present-day requirements.

Dead-eyes are made from lignum vitae, belaying pins from greenheart and 650 blocks from ash or elm. The capstans are of Australian hardwood. In some places laminated wood has been employed, and there are sham fittings not intended for use. Even so the replica went through her paces as efficiently as her prototype would have done, at times despising the use of her twin diesels and certainly not taking advantage of the electronic navigational aids that had been installed.

Had it been possible for Captain Bligh to have sailed in this *Bounty* he would surely have reiterated his words* when he wrote, 'I have the happiness to tell you my little ship does wonderfully well.'

*Bligh to his wife's uncle, Duncan Campbell, 1788.

On the lines of a shallow draught New Zealand trading ketch, Ralph Sewell's *Ripple* is named after the vessel that once sailed on the Manukau (Hauraki Gulf 1973)

Ralph Sewell's miniature *Endeavour* sails in the wake of Cook, Mercury Bay and *left* off Takapuna. *Right*, on the Waitemata in waters denied to Cook by headwinds (1969)

Endeavour II. The Canadian barque took part in the re-enactment of Cook's landing at Botany Bay. The vessel was later wrecked off Parengarenga while on its way to Auckland (Sydney 1970)

The *Bounty* (Bream Bay 1979)

The *Bounty* replica was built by the Whangarei Engineering Company at Whangarei. She is seen here manned by boys who had received training in the *Spirit of Adventure*

A change in the offing

The *Bounty*, romping home

Yachts and Yachting

MANY OF US today become more closely acquainted with the sea through yachting and a marine photographer must at some time or other capture some of the beauty and excitement of this sport. The yacht photographs reproduced here were all taken in or about Auckland's Waitemata Harbour, an area renowned for its yachting.

The *Ariki*, only recently retired from racing, is the senior yacht of the old 'A' class on the Waitemata. The Maori name for 'chief' is an appropriate one, as the *Ariki* has had many a good fight racing her contemporaries. The oldtimer was built in 1904 by the Logan Brothers, who had earned fame as boatbuilders not only in Auckland but throughout the South-west Pacific. The *Ariki*, fifty-four feet overall and retaining her original gaff rig, is seen from the weather quarter while racing in Rangitoto Channel.

The *Ranger* brought new dimensions to New Zealand yachting in the late 1930s. Sixty feet overall, she consistently showed her wake to the rest of Auckland's keelers until she in turn lost pride of place to new design and construction. The photograph has caught the *Ranger's* wake as she passes by during an Anniversary Day regatta on the Waitemata.

The *Kahurangi*, at sixty-two feet overall, is one of New Zealand's largest yachts and was perhaps the first to offer any real challenge to the *Ranger's* supremacy. As can be judged from the photograph of the yacht racing in dirty nor'easter conditions, the *Kahurangi* is a powerful craft. Her activities have not been confined to home waters as she has taken part in ocean racing and deep-sea voyaging.

The *Buccaneer*, seventy-three feet overall, with her light ply construction, when launched superseded all other craft as glamour boat on the Waitemata. Harbour events are just plain sailing for this big cutter, and to prove herself as an allrounder she has cruised deep-sea and taken part in ocean races such as the Pacific Coast-Honolulu classic and the gruelling Sydney-Hobart race, an outstanding test of endurance for both yacht and crew.

In recent years One-tonners have come to the fore as an international class. New Zealand has had some measure of success with these yachts and their crews are well able to hold their own against overseas competitors. In 1971 Aucklander Chris Bouzaid won the coveted One-ton Cup off Heligoland with his *Rainbow II*. The trophy has since gone to Australia and beyond, but yachts like those photographed at the start of a race on the Waitemata will continue to present strong competition in international contests.

The *Piere Lapin* is a Javelin class fourteen-foot yacht raced with a two-man crew. In an exciting duel on the Waitemata a capsize has given the advantage to *Piere Lapin*, which has surged ahead in a smother of spray leaving the vanquished crew floundering.

American yachts are often seen in New Zealand waters, so giving us the opportunity to admire some fine examples of the ship-carver's art. *La Belle Sole* of Los Angeles carries the traditional bald eagle on her transom, which is pictured being refurbished while the yacht is under overhaul on an Auckland slipway. In contrast, the San Francisco schooner *Marie Celine* bears a simple representation of rope twist that surrounds finely executed lettering, the whole so exquisite in its simplicity.

In the late 1930s many of Auckland's A class yachts still carried gaff mains'ls. The *Marangi* (A21), *Tuatea (A20), Victory* (A8) and *Rainbow* (A7) are ahead of the *Moana* at the start of the 1938 Auckland Anniversary Day Regatta. *Below*, the veteran *Ariki* in the Hauraki Gulf (1969)

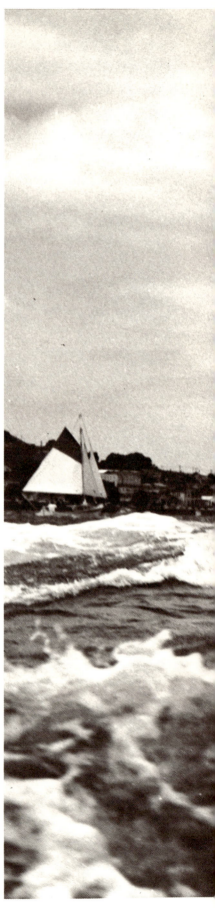

Kahurangi in unpleasant weather (off Rangitoto 1961). *Right*,
a tuck in the mains'l. *Ranger* on the Waitemata (1973)

One-tonners off Orakei. *Streaker* (2020), *Brer Fox* (1919), *Natelle* (83) (1971). *Below*, shallow draught 'mulleties' were raced hard under gaff mains'ls. *Corona* in the wake of *Starlight* during the 1947 Ponsonby Regatta. *Right*, victor and vanquished. The Javelin class *Piere Lapin* on the Waitemata (1973)

The Takapuna class yachts, popularly called 'zeddies', were designed for junior racing. In 1947 thirty-four entered Auckland's Anniversary Day Regatta. *Left*, from Orakei (1950)

La Belle Sole of Los Angeles and
Marie Celine of San Francisco at
Auckland (1970)

Men of the Sea

Portraiture is a branch of photography that I usually fight shy of although occasionally I have indulged in it, perhaps more in the capacity of a snapshotter. If not perfect as portraits, these photographs are treasured for the memories they revive.

Captain Peter Petersen is pictured aboard the logging scow *Rangi* in 1933. Because he had been in the scow *Tally Ho*, Petersen was known as Tally Ho Peter. At the helm is Alan Leyland, who often made voyages in the Leyland O'Brien scow. Never was there such a happy-go-lucky individual, and his presence in this photograph brings back memories of a coastal voyage that cannot be repeated as not a single logging scow remains. Captain Petersen lost his life when the *Rangi* was wrecked in the Hauraki Gulf in 1937.

Captain Collier was photographed aboard the barque *Pamir* on the last leg of her final voyage under the New Zealand ensign. Horace Collier had served under sail, so it was appropriate that he should take command of the *Pamir* when the opportunity arose in 1946. Captain Collier joined the barque at Wellington and sailed for Lyttelton to load for Sydney. On returning to Wellington preparations were made for that remarkable voyage to London and back to New Zealand from Antwerp.

The story of the *Pamir's* seizure at Wellington during World War II is well known. I had previously photographed her arriving at Auckland under Erikson's flag in 1938 but it was not until 1946 that I was again able to follow the barque with a camera. That was when she sailed from Wellington for Vancouver while under the management of the Union SS Company. The next time I was to witness her under sail was when she made that magnificent entry into the Waitemata at the end of the voyage to Europe in 1948. Captain Collier had chosen one of my photographs of this occasion for his personal Christmas card, but he died before it went to the printers. I will ever be thankful to this master for affording me the

Tales of Marco Polo (Deira, United Arab Emirates 1967)

174

opportunity to sail out of Auckland with him, even though it was little more than a drift.

Andrew Thomson, the last of the Southseamen, was master of the schooner *Tiare Taporo* which was built in Auckland by the renowned Charles Bailey Jnr. Andy never sought publicity, and although several journalists attempted to coerce him into divulging his secret past they did not really succeed in extracting much. At first I was more interested in the schooner, which I went over with a tape measure in order to make an accurate plan of the vessel. I came to be on very good terms with Andy and one day a friend, Neil Robinson, and I went down to the *Tiare* and our host opened up a bottle of his best Jamaican rum. We learned of his start in life in New York and his coming to the Pacific, which so captivated him that he never had any desire to leave it. Rarotonga became his home where his wife ran a plantation at Arorangi. Andy's rum was almost my undoing for, on leaving the schooner, there was that queer feeling of walking on air already setting in.

The photograph of the *Tiare Taporo* was taken on another escapade when it looked as though I might have to make an unscheduled trip to Rarotonga with Andy. Fortunately the launch that was to pick up another photographer and myself did manage to catch up with us halfway to Tiri, and all was well.

One who roams the world in the name of the Peace movement is David Moodie, owner of the ketch *Fri*. He is seen sailing out of Auckland on a trip to the Great Barrier with that remarkable Gulf identity Ralph Sewell at the helm — both obviously happy to be in the element they love so dearly. I last heard of David being in Mozambique, and Ralph is planning something bigger and better than his *Ripple*, although it seems impossible that he could improve on his present homely ketch.

Ove Linner also makes a fine study aboard his *Klaraborg*. This was a most difficult low-angle shot because of the restricted deck space between binnacle and bulwark. Ove comes from Gothenburg and went to sea as an engineer with the Swedish East Asiatic Company, but one day he had the opportunity to become part-owner of the old Baltic trader of which he is now the sole owner. In the Solomon Islands the lure of the Pacific has proved so strong that Ove has no desire to return to his homeland.

The most jolly master of a ship I ever met was Esthov Rayer of Tuticorin. Esthov is the owner of the *Mary Isabel* as well as one other thoni, and the portrait was taken between Calicut and Beypore on the Malabar Coast of India. Like his crew, the master is a devout Roman Catholic. Indeed, upon a small altar in the bows below deck a wick burns continuously in a receptacle of coconut oil to illuminate an image of the Virgin Mary.

Sons of Sinbad (Dubai, United Arab Emirates 1967)

Abed al Emmam of the dhow
Fardos (Kuwait 1972) and *below*,
Mohamid Ahmad Najim, nakhoda
of the Omani dhow *Jadakarim*
(Mombasa 1972)

At Pwakuu, Mombasa (1972).
Below, Esthov Rayer. Master-owner
of the Tuticorin thoni *Mary Isabel*
(off Calicut 1973)

Seaman Rogerson of the barque *Pamir* (Hauraki Gulf 1948). *Above*, Captain Andrew (Andy) Thomson of the schooner *Tiare Taporo* (Hauraki Gulf 1962). *Left*, Captain Peter Petersen of the scow *Rangi* with Alan Leyland at the helm (Bay of Plenty 1934)

David Moodie aboard his *Fri* with Ralph Sewell at the helm (Auckland — Great Barrier Island 1972). *Below*, Captain Horace S. Collier aboard the *Pamir* (Hauraki Gulf 1948). *Below right*, Ove Linner. Master-owner of the Swedish ketch *Klaraborg* (1977)

Index